Date due

QUIET OLD, GLASGOW.

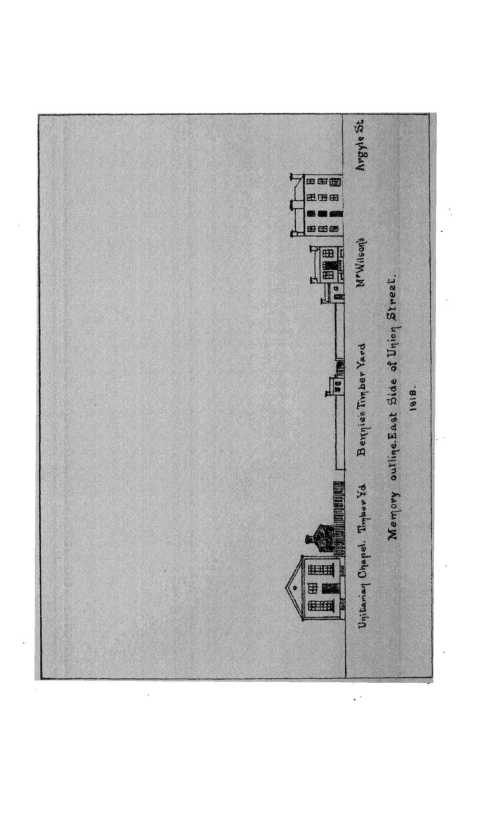

Unitarian Chapel. Timber Yd.   Bennie's Timber Yard   Mc Wilson's   Argyle St

Memory outline. East Side of Union Street.

1818.

QUIET OLD GLASGOW:

ITS

LATTER DAYS BEFORE RAILWAYS,

WITH

Many other interesting matters, giving a Pleasing Account of the Village of

GRAHAMSTON,

which was situate on that part of Argyle Street then known as Anderston Walk,

BY A

BURGESS OF GLASGOW,

Author of "Jamaica Street and Round About in the Year 1820."

GLASGOW:

ROBERT LINDSAY & CO., 81 JAMAICA STREET.

1893.

Hay Nisbet & Co., Printers, 25 Jamaica Street, Glasgow,

AND

169, Fleet Street, London.

"A generous and kindly criticism is always due the local Historian, however modest and unassuming his contribution may be."

"The foundation-stones of all History are those prepared and hewn by the writers of local Histories, and when those Histories are purely the results of the Author's own observation, a chronicle of events and occurrences that have taken place and passed before him in his own time, faithfully and truly narrated, they become sources of pleasure, satisfaction, and usefulness to a long posterity."

Our Author has here strictly and faithfully given the results of his own observation and knowledge. His only book of reference has been the microphone of memory, rolled away back to his own early days, before railways had created the present-day stir and bustle.

QUIET OLD GLASGOW:

ITS

LATTER DAYS BEFORE RAILWAYS.

IT may be interesting to note the great changes that have taken
place in and around the city of Glasgow on its progress to what
it now is, and more especially during the last seventy years.
During these years it has increased and extended more than in
all its previous history, and has, as it were, changed its position
and moved on to the west, and in doing so has blotted out and
swept away many lovely scenes and places of interest once
endeared to the minds of former generations.

On till about 1816, all the churches, public buildings, places
of amusement, etc., and all the dwellings of the wealthier
classes, extended no farther than Buchanan Street, while beyond Union Street were green fields and gardens from the
village of Grahamston on to the village of Anderston, and a
little farther up toward the north, the ground rose up into a
very high hill, called "Harley's Hill," named so from the previous proprietor, Mr. William Harley, who, besides many other
enterprises in which he was engaged for the benefit of the city,
had commenced and laid out the streets for a new town to be
built on the hill; some of the streets at the base had been
formed and partly built upon, when he was compelled to
abandon the whole scheme, owing to the universal stagnation
in trade and commerce which took place after the Peace of
1815-16.

From the summit of the hill a view of the whole country
could be had ; what a treat it was for a family, at the then west
end of the city, to get spending a holiday on the top of "Harley's
Hill," and sitting down to a pic-nic, on a small scale, enjoying
the view all round, looking down on the river with its scanty
shipping and irregular curves along the banks for many miles
down, then turning round and viewing the extensive shipping
at Port Dundas, and wondering how the ships got there, as
there was no water to be seen from this point, and the Campsie
range of hills in the distance.   Turning to the east and looking
far into the country, not intercepted by such clouds of smoke as
are now, might be seen the outlines of "Tintock Tap" and all
the country round ; to the west the lofty Benlomond and
Argyllshire hills, all combined to form a grand and magnificent
scene, well worth coming from a distance to look upon.

The hill, however, was not very much frequented.   The
Glasgow Green' and round about Rutherglen being then the
great holiday resort for the inhabitants of the city.   There can-
not now be got from the same locality such a view as was got
in those days, the hill is now very much lower than it was,
having been levelled down to admit of the formation of Garden
Square (now Blythswood Square), and the immense mass of
earth removed, and used in the formation of streets leading up
from Blythswood Holm and Sauchiehall Road, now

SAUCHIEHALL STREET.

This was then a quiet, pleasant road, far removed from the
noise and bustle of the city, having here and there a few rustic
cottages placed by the roadside, where refreshments could be
got.   These houses were very much frequented at holiday and
other times by the families and youths from the city who
travelled out to enjoy the "curds and cream and fruits in their

seasons," which were always to be had there. There was one of these cottages had fallen into bad repute ; it had at one time, like the others, its nice garden and very cosy bowers; it was situated at the east end, in the vicinity of where a numerous body of tradesmen were employed in the formation and building of streets ; it was called the "Fish," from having a long spire with a large fish on the top; it had been degraded into a common public-house, frequented chiefly by those of the workmen who chose to misspend their money in that way.

Some years previous to this time (1820) it was the usual custom for genteel families residing in and around Stockwell Street to have their summer quarters out in this direction, in farm and other houses, about the termination of this road, and a little farther to the north, about the end of Dobbie's Loan ; and here, among others who came to spend a day with their friends in their summer residences, were the family of Mr. Wyld, a merchant who had a self-contained house and garden in Stockwell Street, nearly opposite the Goosedubbs ; he was the first to establish a branch of the Commercial Bank of Scotland in the city ; the bank offices were in his own place of business, and for a time he used to carry the cash and books of the bank home with him to his own dwelling, bringing them out in the mornings.

Passing along Sauchiehall Road toward the west, a little beyond the base of "Harley's Hill"—which on that side had a very steep ascent to the top—a quiet country road turned down to the left, on one side of which was a large sheet of water known as "Gillespie's Pond"—very much resorted to in winter for sliding and skating—passing which was the upper end of North Street, leading down to the village of Anderston.

This village derived its name from Mr. Anderson of Stobcross, by whom it was laid out, and began to be formed on one of his farms about 1725. It was originally occupied almost wholly by weavers, whose houses of two storeys—consisting of dwelling-house above and loom-shop below—with two or three small mansions, surrounded by large gardens, formed the Main Street on either side of the highway to Dumbarton. It did not make much progress until about the beginning of the present century, when steam power began to be applied to machinery. A spinning mill and two or three power-loom factories were erected, so that in 1802 the population was 4462, and from this time it continued extending and increasing until before 1830 it had a provost and bailies and a police office.

GRAND SPECTACLE—" BAY OF NAPLES" IN GLASGOW.

During the autumn and part of the winter of 1837 there was a grand exhibition got up at the west end of Anderston on Cranstonhill. It consisted of a representation of the City and Bay of Naples, with the eruption of Mount Vesuvius in the distance. It was on a large scale, having a plentiful supply of water from the reservoir of the Cranston Hill Water-works to form the waters of the Bay, and the lights from the houses shining on the waters made a grand scene ; the eruption, which was produced every night by fireworks and other explosives, had at times rather an alarming effect on the minds of some of the audience. The walks of the surrounding grounds being lined with small globular lamps, with others suspended from the branches of trees, made the whole affair a most magnificent scene.

The boundary of Anderston on the east was a small burn, separating it from Blythswood estate. Bishop Street is next to the boundary ; the name is derived from this being one of the routes of the Bishops of Glasgow, through country roads, from the Cathedral to and from the summer residence, which stood on the east bank of the Kelvin, about two hundred yards from the river Clyde.   It was a dark, gloomy-looking building, with bleak, barren surroundings, more like a ruined fortress than a summer house for Bishops.   It was known as the "Bishop's Castle."   The walls were still standing quite firm up till about 1818, or perhaps a few years further on, when it was taken down.   On the east side of what is now Bishop Street, about half-way up, running east and west, stood a row of old brick buildings, known as the "Beggars' Raw."   This was said to be the place where the poor assembled to get the blessing and the alms of the Bishops, as they passed and repassed on their way through Blythswood grounds, where was a terrace and road shaded by large trees.   Running parallel to and on the south side of what is now Bothwell Terrace, and passing along the upper end of the village of Grahamston, a road led on to four or five detached country houses or villas, from whence they could pass on to the Cathedral by the High Street or Rottenrow.

FYFE PLACE—A GHOST STORY.

These country houses stood on the south side of what is now Fyfe Place, West George Street, fronting the north, and having gardens at the back.   For some two or three years previous to these houses being taken down, the one at the west end was not occupied, the windows were broken, the garden in desolation, and the whole premises got into a ruinous state. A report got abroad that the house was haunted by the "Ghost" of a lady dressed in black!   The grounds round about were frequented as a playground by boys and lads from Melville Street and Drury Lane, but none of them would ever venture near the haunted house after nightfall.   One afternoon, towards the gloaming, some of them, tired with their play, sat down to chat about the haunted house and the ghost.   Some of the boys said they were not afraid of ghosts ; the others dared them to try and go into the house just now. Being thus put to the test, three or four of the boldest rose, went through the garden, pushed open the door, which was not secured, went bravely in ; and for a time shouts of defiance were heard throughout the house, then a lull, then a wild shout of terror, and then the boys came rushing out in great alarm, crying they had seen the ghost ! All the others came crowding round to hear what they had seen—some mocking and jeering, others in great alarm, and all looking earnestly toward the open door— when a lady, dressed in black, appeared in the doorway. She stood gazing all around for about three minutes, never opening her mouth, then stretched out her right arm, with clenched hand, shook it, and departed, closing the door behind her. The crowd of boys and lads fled in terror, and there was no more play that night. Some of the people in the house adjoining had taken this plan to frighten them, and it had that effect for some time.

NEW BRITISH SYSTEM OF EDUCATION.

Returning to the foot of Bishop Street and passing eastward to the city by Anderston Walk, there stood a very large academy and play grounds occupying the whole space between M'Alpine and Carrick Street. On the front of the building was painted, in large letters, " New British System of Education." There were two entrances to the building, one for the females only, from Carrick Street, having a range of offices at the back, separating them from that portion of the ground used by the males. A railing divided the large plot of play-ground in front, and the entrance for all males was by M'Alpine Street only, thus the boys and girls each used their own portion of the grounds for their various games. The interior of the building was one large hall with lofty ceiling, and large platform about six feet high at the end next M'Alpine Street, on the front of this were the desks of the masters, who had thus a sort of bird's eye view of every class and corner throughout the whole school. Behind these were placed chairs and large tables, with globes, for the use of the pupils studying geography, etc. Every branch of education was taught, from the alphabet up to the highest, by Mr. Boyd and his active assistant, Mr. Speirs. The alphabet was taught in a very peculiar manner by the use of what was called the "sand desk." This was a long narrow desk or table, having a space on front about nine inches wide and one inch deep, with a sliding board nine inches square fitted to run in this space, which was covered with very fine sand about one fourth of an inch deep. An enclosed wheel, having the whole of the alphabet painted on it, showing one letter at a time in a square space at the top, was placed in the front of the platform, about the middle of, and opposite to, the desk. The monitor took his stand in front of the class of pupils, and then turning the wheel to A, would say, Now, this is the first letter, it is named A, now look at it, there are two lines stretching out and meeting at the top and another line across, now then, write the letter on the sand with your finger instantly. A dozen or so of busy fingers and eager faces were down, every one anxious to produce the form of the letter shown. When this was done, and the letters examined by the monitor, the sliding board was run along the sand and a smooth surface formed for the next letter. There were many curious figures formed before getting through the alphabet. But the pupils, being interested in the process, very soon learned, having to print every letter on the sand it became imprinted on the mind.

The sand desk was also the place of punishment for the juniors, which was always done by Mr. Boyd personally. The

case was ever carefully inquired into before this was done, then
the culprit was brought to the desk, the bell was rung, silence
was called, and lessons suspended. Mr. Boyd stated the case
to the whole school, then taking hold of the offender tenderly,
yet firmly, laid him across the desk, bottom upwards, gave him
a few smart strokes with a pair of good "Scotch taws" on that
part of the body specially adapted to receive such impressions.

The girls in the junior classes were punished in a different
manner, being made to stand up, separated from the class, for a
longer or shorter time, according to the nature of the offence.
The whole school was conducted in a most orderly, systematic
manner—juniors divided into classes, headed by a monitor from
among themselves, Mr. Speirs constantly going among these
and the higher branches ; while Mr. Boyd from the platform—
where he taught the scientific classes—overlooked the whole.
The first exercise in the morning was the reading of a portion
of the Bible all round in the classes. Everyone was kept strictly
to their lessons during school hours, which were not long—from
ten till three, with an interval for play from twelve till one—on
Saturdays from ten till twelve. The holidays were few, and
never longer than two days at a time. The great carnival
holiday of the year was Candlemas Day, about which more may
be said. Mr. Harley's two sons and many of the families of the
merchants of the city received their education at this academy.

Passing along Anderston Walk—on either side of which
were stunted hedges, with here and there small plots of kitchen
garden, rudely enclosed with paling—and turning up into what
is now Mains Street—then a pleasant, retired walk between
rows of high hedges, leading past the upper part of the village
of Grahamston, with its starching work, brewery, etc., and
terminating near to what is now the lower end of Renfield
Street, on the east side of which stood a large granary five

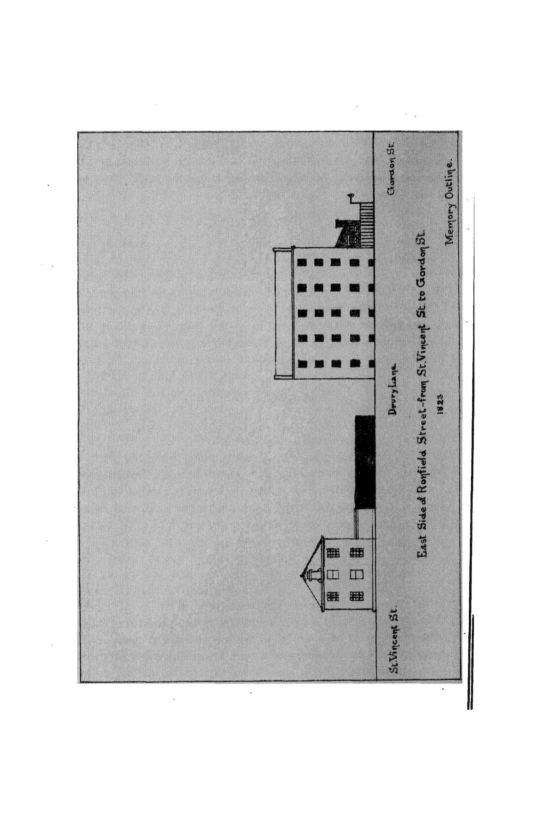

St.Vincent St.

Drury Lane.

Gordon St.

East Side of Renfield Street—from St.Vincent St. to Gordon St.

1823

Memory Outline.

storeys high—this, including a cabinetmaker's workshop, at the corner of what was Melville Street, occupied the whole space up to Drury Lane.

DRURY STREET.

This name originated through a whim of two young lads— one a painter, the other a printer—who resided in the lane about 1819. They had been reading about Drury Lane and Drury Lane Theatre in London, and, thinking the large Independent Chapel at the corner, where Mr. Greville Ewing's earnest preaching brought crowds to hear him from all parts, would be like the theatre there, they resolved to give it that name. Getting a strong sheet of paper well painted and lettered "Drury Lane," a ladder was procured, and late on Saturday evening it was fixed up on the opposite corner of the chapel. Hundreds read it next day. The paper stood the weather for more than a year, and when the streets came to be regularly lettered it got the name, Drury Street.

Crossing St. Vincent Street and passing along the road, on the line of what is now the east side of Renfield Street, stood an old boundary hedge about five feet high, the stems of which were so close, and the branches so intertwined with each other, that it formed nearly a level on the top, on which boys used to walk for some considerable distance. Further on, after crossing Sauchiehall Road, was a large freestone quarry, which had not been wrought for many years, and was known as the "Cowcaddens Quarry." It extended from Cambridge Lane, near the base of Garnet Hill, eastward, on to Port Dundas Road, and through a tunnel under the road, was worked some distance beyond it, and from the north side of Sauchiehall Road, on to the boundary of Cowcaddens, where it terminated in a perpendicular face of rock about twenty-five feet high.

During the years in which the quarry was being filled up this rock was a great resort for members of some of the volunteer corps that had been got up during the Radical rising, and had not yet been disbanded. Here they came to exercise their skill as marksmen, having targets painted on the face of the rock; and here also came boys to gather the flattened lead bullets they had been using. It was rather a dangerous occupation, as the bullets sometimes rebounded farther, and went in directions they had not calculated upon.

In the course of working the quarry about 1819, near the west end, about the middle, and several feet below the surface, the workmen came upon a large fossil tree having all the larger limbs still attached. It was an object of great interest to geologists, and many came from all parts of the city and elsewhere to see it, and carry off fragments whenever they could get the opportunity.

Some distance from the west end of this quarry, and on the base of the north side of Garnethill, stood the old powder magazine, then far removed from every dwelling, and used for the purpose of storing all the gun powder belonging to merchants and dealers in that article, who were allowed to keep only a very small quantity on their premises in the city.

THE VILLAGE OF GRAHAMSTON.

Reference has already been made to the village of Graham's Town or Grahamston. It was not known from whom the name was derived, and may be quite new to many who were well acquainted with all the villages at one time joining the suburbs of the city. There was, however, a village of that name, which extended from the west side of Union Street on to the west side of Hope Street, and from the north side of Argyle Street up to above the line of Gordon Street. It consisted of one street (Alston) running south and north, and a lane at the south end on the west side leading into various buildings at the back. Beyond these, and occupying the remaining portion of the grounds connected with them, were kitchen gardens let out to gardeners, who raised up vegetables to supply the markets in the city. In the Glasgow Directory of 1789 there are the names of six market gardeners, which was a large proportion of the trades of the village. The buildings fronting Union Street and along the north side of Argyle Street, including a large cartwright work belonging to M. Norris near to the boundary, were all included in the village, on the west side of which was a large granary, next to that a brewery, and a little farther up a large sugar refinery; opposite this on the east side were two very large, old granaries, and above these the starch works of Mr. Lockhart.

In the front tenement on the west side, looking into Argyle Street, was the residence of Mr. Marshall, the village school-master, whose class-room or school-house was on the opposite side of the street, in Dallas Court. Nearly all the villagers, and many from other places, attended his school. He was a very careful, painstaking teacher, and would never think of advancing his pupils into any higher branch until they had a perfect knowledge of what they were then engaged in. He had a peculiar method of punishment. There were no steel pens as yet invented; much of the teacher's time during the writing classes was occupied in making and mending pens. Then was the time for boys working sly mischief with each other, and then was the time for the master watching them. He kept hanging over his desk two old brown wigs and a large pair of tawse, and setting his back to the desk, and his eyes every now and then looking over his spectacles. Whenever he saw anything wrong going on, he calmly took down the tawse, threw them over to the offender, ordering him to bring them up. Then taking down one of the old wigs, placed it on his head, and with his right forefinger in his ear, and the left one in his mouth, set him marching through the school-room, a most ludicrous object. This mode of punishment was very trying to the feelings of a sensitive youth, and especially so if he had a sweetheart among the girls, amidst whom he must pass during his march.

Among the brief but merry holidays which all the schools had, none were looked forward to with more interest and excitement than that of Candlemas Day; it was on this day all the schools—high and low—presented the Candlemas offering to their teachers, and it was looked forward to by many a poor teacher, well educated men, struggling to obtain a living in a profession which was then very poorly paid. This offering was sums of money given to the teachers by all their scholars, varying in amount from threepence to five shillings, and from two shillings up to ten, according to the status of the schools and the position of the parents. Those pupils who gave the highest sums being king or queen of the day, and for some time after.

The school met that day at the usual hour, all tidily dressed, but no lesson books. A table had been placed in front of the master's desk on which was a large basket of oranges, and it might be a few packages of sweeties. When all were seated in their respective places, the master took his stand behind the table, and, after a few complimentary words, began to call out the names, when each stepped up and presented their offering, receiving in return an orange or two, according to the amount of offering. All went on with quietness and decorum till the names of the king and queen were called out, then there was a rush towards them, the boys to carry the king, and the girls the queen shoulder high through the school; after that, mirth and merriment—the boys "pappin' peas" at each other, a supply of these having been provided and kept in the pockets "biding the time." There was no fear of the brown wigs, it was a day of liberty, and many an urchin fancied himself a hero, "pappin peas at the master" without fear of the consequence, and yet terrified at his own temerity.

A THEATRE IN THE VILLAGE OF GRAHAMSTON.

The first regular theatre in Scotland, excepting one established in Edinburgh about eighteen years previous, was built in the village of Grahamston in 1764. It stood fronting the street, and along the lane behind the tenement in which Mr. Marshall had his residence.

The circumstances which led to its being erected in this place were these. After the Reformation, plays and theatrical representations of all kinds were strictly prohibited, and denounced by the ministers of the Gospel throughout the country from their respective pulpits. The feeling against theatres continued strong in the minds of the ministers and people all throughout Scotland, and especially in the city of Glasgow, down to this time, so that when a company from London came down for the purpose of establishing a theatre in the city, they got no encouragement from the authorities, and no one could be found daring enough to sell a piece of ground for that purpose. Grahamston, being the nearest village out of the bounds of the city—the boundary pillar stood on the west side of Union Place—was next applied to, where a proprietor sought the then very high price of five shillings per square yard for his ground, possibly thinking that such a price would deter them from making a purchase. They, however, agreed to take it at that price, and the building of the theatre was at once gone on with.

2

The erection of the building caused a great sensation among the people in the city and the village, which increased during its progress to completion to that extent of excitement and determination not to allow a theatre, that a short time previous to the day fixed for opening it was set on fire, and a great amount of damage done ; the stage, scenery, actors' wardrobes, etc., being all destroyed.   The building not having suffered much, the damage was repaired, and the theatre at length opened by Mrs. Bellamy, then a popular actress of London. This attempt to destroy the building was hurried on by a preacher in the street who, while denouncing the erection of the building, told his auditors that he dreamed the preceding night that he was in the infernal regions and saw a grand entertainment, at which Lucifer gave a toast in honour of M——, who had sold his ground to build him a house upon.

From this time the theatre was carried on by various companies from London and Edinburgh till April, 1782, when it was burned down, leaving nothing but the walls standing, under circumstances which left no doubt that the people of Glasgow were determined to have no theatre in their neighbourhood.   Dr. Cleland, city architect, and author of "Annals of Glasgow," etc., records having been present during the course of the fire, and of hearing the shouts of the excited mob, and the cries of "Save the ither folks' hooses an' let the d—— hoose burn."

The walls of the building fronting the street being in good condition, were some time after roofed over, and divided and fitted up for stables and other offices ; and the remains of the first theatre in the city were still standing up till the time when the whole village was swept away.

Next to the ruins of the theatre were two tenements of dwelling-houses, and behind these were other buildings and houses, and beyond these a large extent of ground laid out in vegetables for supplying the markets in the city. All these houses, and others on the east side of the street, were chiefly occupied by market gardeners, "granarymen," and carters employed in carting grain from Port Dundas. On either side of the street at this point the buildings were set back about forty feet in a distance of about eighty feet, leaving a large open space, on which stood the carts when work was over; while behind these were stables and dungpits. These carters and "granarymen" were rather a superior class, and were often seen on summer evenings seated on their carts in social converse, or discussing the movements of the Radicals and the possibility of a general rising and overthrow of the Government; and on quiet Sabbath evenings, when all was still—there being no thoroughfare—small family groups might be seen engaged in reading or in serious conversation, while enjoying the pure, fresh air of the street.

On the west, and joining one of the sides of the open space, was a large store or granary connected with an extensive brewery, which had been established here about the year 1743. Previous to this time the manufacture of ale and porter had been carried on in a very small way in the city. This brewery, also other two—one of these stood on the west side of Turner's Court, about mid-way down, and nearly opposite to the "Glasgow Pin Manufactory"—were for the manufacture of small beer, table beer, and porter, the small beer being very much used by the working classes as a beverage and at meals. Butter milk was then scarce, and only to be had at certain times of the year, and even then the supply was very limited. The beer was used chiefly at breakfast, taken with porridge, and formed an excellent and agreeable substitute for milk. The water supply also at that time was very bad, and often tempted the hard-working man to spend a penny on a "bottle of yill," which was a very refreshing drink, and not in the least degree intoxicating. They, however, sometimes went beyond this, and "a gill an' a bottle o' yill an' a lick o' meal" might be heard as the usual order given on going into a public-house. These mixed together made a very refreshing stimulant when taken in moderation, and far superior to the gaseous sodas and brandies of the present day.

A SOBER BREWER.

An incident in connection with this brewery while occupied by Mr. Galway (about 1820), who, with his family, resided on the premises, may here be mentioned as showing the character of the majority of the inhabitants of Grahamston in their respect for the Sabbath. During the attempted rising of the Radicals at this time all the banks in the city were well guarded by private watchmen, well armed. One of these men, who resided in Drury Lane, and who was one of the guard employed in watching the Royal Bank in Queen Street, had met with a severe accident owing to the accidental discharge of a pistol. This occurred late on Saturday night, and when the doctor arrived and had dressed the wound he prescribed " barm poultices " to be applied as soon as possible. Early next morning a neighbour's boy was sent for the barm—which was then sold by the brewers to thrifty housewives while bottling their ale—but on arriving and asking for the barm, the servant who opened the door told him very severely and decidedly he would get no barm here on a Sabbath morning. "But," insisted the boy, "it's for to mak' a poltis tae a man that was shot last nicht when he was watchin' the Radicals." On hearing this, she at once went up and aroused Mr. Galway, who came to the door, and, after a great deal of minute inquiry and "back spearin'," believing the boy to be telling the truth, cheerfully gave him the barm, would not take payment, and told him to come back if more was required.

THE DRINKING CUSTOMS.

The drinking customs and other usages of the country were still very prevalent in and around the city among all classes of society. There was not such a distinction among classes then as there is now, in their manners, mode of living, and residence ; such as people having shops in Trongate, dwelling in the "Burn Close," or men in business in Cochrane Street residing in Drury Lane, others dwelt above their shops in various parts of the city, while many of the city merchants had their residence in the aristocratic suburb lying between Buchanan and North Frederick Streets.

Among the working and middle class, when a baby was born, all the neighbours were invited, or expected to call and get their "Blythe Meat," which consisted of bread and cheese, and a glass of whisky to drink to the health of mother and baby. In connection with this, when the child was carried to church for baptism, by the mother and a friend, a neatly folded parcel of fine bread and cheese was taken with them and presented to the first person they met, who had to turn and walk with the party a short distance on their way to church.

The usual mode of shewing kindness and hospitality to a visitor, by respectable housewives, was by treating them to a dram with sugar and a bit of oatmeal cake, this was then, to a visitor, what a cup of tea is now, and they would have felt slighted had it not been offered to them. Among men in business and neighbouring shopkeepers it was quite common to leave their business about mid-day and go out to get what was called their "meridian," in certain public-houses or "change houses" in the vicinity, and should it so happen that a customer called on business matters with any of these while out, it was not thought the least disrespectable to let it be known where he was, when the party would either cause him to be sent for or call upon him there. Many of the public-houses or small taverns were called "change houses," as during some years when there was a great scarcity of silver coinage, when shopkeepers and others would have their assistants or apprentices running up and down streets for change of a one pound note. These houses always managed to have a supply of silver for the convenience of their customers, and their own profit, as tradesmen often resorted to these houses when settling accounts or paying their workmen, many of whom were often tempted to leave part of their earnings with the "change house." Some of the public houses were labelled, or painted in large letters, "Herb Ale House," where customers of the same class went out to get their "mornin'," which consisted of a tumbler or two of herb ale, prepared every morning, and taken warm, with a glass of whisky bitters stirred into it. This was considered to be a good tonic generally, and in some cases to rectify the over-dose of toddy taken on the previous evening.

It was a general custom among the upper and middle classes to treat tradesmen, who came to work about their houses, with a dram, even after an hour or two of work, and if the work were to occupy a few days, to give them their "meridian" every day. On one occasion, among others of like nature, while a squad of painters were employed in a tenement of respectable houses, a worthy lady, one of the tenants, anxious to have her house finished soon, gave the workmen their dram twice a day, with the result that she was the last in the tenement to get rid of the painters. In some of the wholesale, and in the retail warehouses, a jar of spirits was kept on the premises to treat a customer. But although the drinking habits were thus so very prevalent, there was little drunkenness, and men staggering along the streets and roads in a state of intoxication were very seldom met with.

One reason for this was the spirits were pure and genuine, not adulterated. They were exhilarating, and not of a stupefying or very intoxicating nature till taken to excess. Another reason was that some of those engaged in the trade were conscientious in the sale of the article. Take one instance of this class of worthy men. Two respectable tradesmen would step in on a forenoon, enter the public room, and give their order thus :—" Bring ben a gill o' yer best, Mr.——." " The vera best?" " Oh, yes, the very best." This was brought in, and in about a quarter of an hour the bell rang, and, holding out the pewter measure, one of them would say, " That's gran' stuff o' yours, Mr. ——, bring ben anither fou o' the stoup." He would look at them, say nothing, take it up hesitatingly to obey the order. In about half-an-hour after the bell was rung, the stoup handed over for a fresh supply, with the remark, " That's splendid stuff o' yours." " Aye, it's splendid stuff, but a couldna' gie ye ony mair the noo. Ye've gotten twa gless the piece, and you'll be gettin' mair before nicht, an' I couldna' gie ye anither drap."

SOME STORIES ABOUT THE ROYAL EXCHANGE.

It was a custom—although not quite general—of giving tradesmen an allowance for drink at the erection of a dwelling house or other premises. This was carried out to its fullest extent—and far beyond it—at the building of the Royal Exchange about 1829-30. The tradesmen had already received small sums during the progress of the work, and, when the interior of the building was getting near to completion, all the

floors being laid down, a general invitation was sent to all the
men who had been and were still employed at the building that
a dinner was to be given them on such a day, at two o'clock, and
to come in their working clothes. The large News Room had
been fitted up with seats and tables formed of clean planks.
The men came punctual to the hour—ready for dinner—and as
every man took his seat he was supplied with a glass of spirits,
then a tumbler of porter. A most substantial dinner was set
before them, and, while partaking of it, waiters were busy supplying them with spirits and porter, which the men took without
thinking of the consequences. Immediately after dinner most
of the building committee and some of the contractors, who
were seated on a raised platform, began to give toasts, while
busy waiters were throng filling the men's glasses and tumblers
to enable them to respond. The result was that by about four
o'clock the whole of the men had risen from the tables, and
were "stotterin'" about in a state of hilarious excitement, more
or less according to temperament. The whole affair had been a
plot to bring this about, taking advantage of the men being
invited to dinner. Some of the men felt indignant, others were
ashamed; the majority were well satisfied, and collected next
day around a barrel of porter to finish a quantity of liquor that
still remained of the abundant supply provided for the occasion.

During the progress of the building a very peculiar case of
theft took place, which might have been a very serious matter
for those concerned, at a time when punishment for crime was
very severe. The front portion of the Exchange was built upon
the foundations of the Royal Bank. From the south end on
till beyond the main entrance the walls were not taken down,
and it was while taking down the mason-work of a safe, which
stood in the way of the plans being carried out, two of the men
employed, while turning over a quantity of waste paper in a

corner of the safe, found a large parcel of one pound bank notes of the Royal Bank. The men had hitherto been considered respectable and honest, but here was a great temptation, and they yielded to it, and took possession of the notes. They did not return to their work next day, and for two or three days after were going about, flush of money, drinking and treating their comrades, who were surprised to find them having so much silver money on hand. Suspicion arose, inquiries were made, and, from some hints the men gave during their drinking, the police got notice, and they were apprehended.

The surroundings of the Police Buildings, at the corner of Albion and Bell Streets, were not in a very civilised state at this time. The "Bell Street Mutton Market" stood next to the tenement of buildings fronting Candleriggs, and here might be seen during the day respectable housewives, attended by their servants, making their purchases; while on Saturday afternoons were tradesmen's wives, and on to the latest hour crowds of the poorer class, bargaining for small portions of meat which had been rejected by their wealthier neighbours, and which the fleshers were willing to sell at very reduced prices, in order to have their sometimes perishable stock cleared out. The entrance to the Court-Room was close by the end of the market; and in a large space beyond the Police Buildings were always to be seen a collection of wheelbarrows of various sorts, which had been found perambulating in places and under circumstances which led to their being brought to the office. There were also a number of ladders and other articles, which had been found lying in closes and left about buildings—all waiting for their owners to claim them, if they were worth claiming and paying expenses. The Police Buildings stood nearly on a line with Albion Street, the cells for female prisoners being all on that side, extending down to nearly the line of Bell Street. The

windows looking out on Albion Street were all well secured
with strong iron gratings, and glazed sashes inside; and at
some of these windows on court days, while the prisoners were
waiting to be brought before the magistrate, the windows being
open for ventilation, advantage was taken of this by those
inside, to converse with associates without, who were always
waiting on these occasions on the opposite side of the narrow
street; and the brief conversations that then took place were
the very reverse of everything that is peaceful, modest, and
pure. One outside would shout out in a kind of sympathising
tone, "Ha, Nellie, what are ye in for?" "Nabbin' a ticker;
but I'll do for him yet, the —— !" Another from the inside
would cry out, "Ha, Kirsty, ye ——, I'll dowse your glims
when a win oot, for blabbin' on me, ye —— !" The whole was
a scene of ribaldry, and had a most demoralising effect on the
minds of many of the youth of both sexes who, in passing by
on their errands or business, stayed to listen.

It was through such scenes and surroundings as this the two
tradesmen were brought before the magistrate, to be examined
on a charge of stealing a parcel of bank notes of the Royal
Bank from a safe in the bank. The whole charge against them
somehow or other fell to the ground. The notes were not
stolen from a safe in the Royal Bank, as it was then the Royal
Exchange. The notes were not bank notes, but only a parcel
of forged ones, which had been thrown into a corner of the safe
to be burned along with the waste paper. The men were
discharged, but with a very much blemished character; and
the only parties who suffered loss were the publicans who so
very kindly provided the silver money, and for whom very little
sympathy was felt.

A very ingenious fraud and daring robbery was perpetrated
on the Royal Bank a few years previous to its removal. About

mid-day a splendid equipage came leisurely driving up the then quiet Queen Street, and halted at one of the gates of the bank, which had a parapet wall, with ornamental railings above, on the line of Queen Street, with a gate at each end. A circular stair from each of these gates led to a large landing-place, on which were the principal entrances to the bank. The equipage consisted of an open carriage, with postillion, in which was seated an aristocratic - looking personage, with one or two footmen in livery seated behind. The whole was distinctly seen from the windows of the bank, so that when the occupier of the carriage came into the bank, with all the necessary credentials, and presented a draft or order for a very large amount from a bank either in Edinburgh or London—it is not known which—it was at once paid without the least suspicion. There was no telegraph or telephone then, postal communication was slow, and before either bank could be advised with, the robbers had got clear off with their booty.

THE BURNING OF THE THEATRE-ROYAL IN QUEEN STREET.

It was while the building of the Exchange was going on that the Theatre-Royal in Queen Street was entirely destroyed by fire. It stood between St. Vincent Street and what is now the north side of Exchange Square, having a splendid frontage to Queen Street, about seventy feet wide, and extended back about 158 feet, or on to St. Vincent Place, which then consisted of only three or four self-contained houses, with offices and green behind, enclosed by brick walls. The then east house belonged to and was occupied by Mr. Robert Dalglish, who was Lord Provost of the city during the passing of the Reform Bill. All the ground behind these houses, on to the walls of the garden behind the Royal Bank, and westward to Buchanan Street, was a wilderness, and a "free coup" for all sorts of building rubbish.

The interior of the theatre was very spacious and lofty, consisting of two tiers of boxes, pit, first and second gallery, which brought the audience in the latter to a great height above the stage. Over and above the scenery was a large loft, the full extent of the width of the building, having spaces for carpenters' benches, etc., etc., and a space left for the rolling along of a strong wooden cylinder, having a number of lead balls inside, which was brought into use when the performance included a thunderstorm. On the front part of the building, between the staircases at each end, and above the main entrance, was a small hall and side rooms, the hall was used for teaching elocution and dancing classes, etc., and sometimes for the training in the "noble art of self-defence," as the brutal practice was then called.

The fire began in the theatre on the forenoon, shortly after the rehearsal of the play for the evening performance, and there was soon a scene of great excitement among the numerous workmen at the Exchange and all around the locality. The contractor for the wright work, Mr. William Binnie, had a large quantity of prepared timber piled up close to the wall of the theatre. This, his men, with the assistance of others, got removed to a place of safety. After this—there being no other property in danger, the side walls of the building being rather higher than the adjacent property on the north side—a number of the men went to assist at the fire engines, partly in the expectation of getting a premium or reward for their services, which was then sometimes given to persons coming to assist at fires. In this case there were too many came forward, and rather hindered than helped the firemen in their efforts to extinguish the flames, now spreading rapidly, until the roof fell in ; and before five o'clock in the afternoon there was nothing left of the once grand theatre but four bare, naked, scorched walls.

Opposite to the theatre, but a little further down, were the premises of Mr. Henry Lawson, who was the first, or among the first, to introduce cabs into the city. The sedan chair was gradually going out of fashion, but remained in use a few years longer. The last "Sedan Chair Office" was in Drury Street. On the front of Mr. Lawson's grocery and victualling shop was a small, modest-looking board, on which was inscribed, "One-Horse Coach Office." These machines were at first called "noddys," owing to their construction; the two wheels attached to the trams, and by springs on which the carriage rested, caused a jolting, nodding motion to the passengers while going along over the sometimes very rough causeway.

Next to Mr. Lawson's, at the corner of Ingram Street, stood the old Gaelic kirk. It was a plain, substantial building, standing back about seven or eight feet, and having a neat stone wall about eight feet high on the line of the streets. The entrance was from Ingram Street, by a gate about five feet wide, on either side of which were covered porches, where the elders stood with the plates before them to receive the offerings of the people as they came in to worship.

On the opposite corner of Ingram and Queen Streets stood a large sugar-house, or sugar refinery, extending down Queen Street a little farther than what is now the south side of Exchange Square. There were four sugar-houses in and around the city about the year 1680, two of these in the vicinity of Gallowgate and High Street, and one in the village of Grahamston, which has yet to be noticed.

For some years previous to the Exchange being built building operations were entirely at a stand in the then West End of the city. There were a great many vacant steadings of ground in the surrounding streets. The south side of George Square had only a tenement at the north-east corner and one at the west end, while a large wooden erection—a rotunda or panorama—occupied part of the vacant ground between. At the corner of the Square and Queen Street were the cabinet workshops and timber yards of Messrs. White, and large spaces of vacant ground—some of them partly occupied by temporary workshops, mason and slate yards, etc.—were still remaining in Buchanan, Melville, and Mitchell Streets.

Within a few years after the building of the Exchange, and even when the Square around it was being built, a gradual change began over the whole locality, buildings of various descriptions were being erected, and the vacant ground filled up; and in Buchanan Street, where on the east side toward Argyle Street was a range of handsome dwellings, elevated above the street, having gardens between and the high brick walls behind, covered with fruit trees; while farther up, on the west side, were family dwellings, a little elevated above the street, which was there so quiet and retired that family groups might be seen on a summer evening sipping their tea at the open window. A gradual change came over all this, and in a very few years the once aristocratic Buchanan Street was entirely occupied by shops, warehouses, and offices.

GEORGE SQUARE.

On to about 1819 George Square was a quiet and very retired locality. The interior of the Square was a green without trees or shrubbery, enclosed all round with a plain iron railing four feet high, and a gate opposite the head of Miller Street. Inside on the green were always to be seen a number of sheep wandering about, nibbling at the stunted grass, looking very dull and far from being satisfied with their surroundings. The Square lay entirely out of the line of business, except when on some occasions the Lords of the Circuit Court took up their residence in the George Inn, at the east end of the Square. Then there were crowds so long as they remained, and it was rather a strange sight to many who came to see the guard of soldiers pacing to and fro in front of the inn.

There was another slight traffic through the Square on Saturdays—boys and men, bird fanciers and others, on their way from the surrounding villages to attend the Bird Market, which for some years was held at the east end of Cochrane Street, on the north side, along the dead wall of the brewery in Montrose Street; and here, affixed to the wall, were rows of cages hung up, containing a variety of birds; while along, and seated on the kerbstone, were young lads and boys with baskets and boxes of various sorts, in which were rabbits, pup dogs, white mice, etc. It was a lively scene on a summer day, with the singing and chirruping of the birds and the chaffering and sometimes noisy arguments used by the merchant to describe the pure genealogy of the animals and birds they were anxious to get rid of.

The beginning of what brought George Square to be what it now is was the erection of the monument and statue of General Sir John Moore, a few yards within the iron railing, and opposite Miller Street, in the year 1819. In the summer of that year the people in the vicinity, and the very few passers by, had their curiosity excited by seeing a large number of strong wooden boxes being laid down at the gate opposite Miller Street; some of these large and square, others smaller, and of different shapes and angles, the whole of them were each secured and fastened with strong iron clasps at the corners. They lay there a few days before being opened, and during that time groups of prentice lads and others from Drury Lane and Grahamston assembled round the mysterious boxes at meal hours, and in evenings discussing and speculating what might be in them, and why they had been laid down there. It was such an unusual sight to be seen in the then quiet square. At last two of the boys, who had been making inquiry, were able to tell that "they were gaun to mak' a monument to a great General they ca'd Moore, that was shot whun he was fechtin wi' the French awa' in Spain, an' a' the pieces o' the monument an' himsel was in the boxes, and that when he was a chap like oursels he stoppit wi' his feyther doon in Miller Street, and that was the wye they were buildin' the monument up here, that he micht be lookin' doon the street whaur he leev'd when he was a wee chap."

This information satisfied the audience in the meantime, and then, while seated on the boxes, an earnest conversation might take place about battles, and fighting the French, and the possibility of some of them getting monuments to their memory, like the chap that lived down in Miller Street, till the sound of the bell, or the cry of the night watchman, "Past ten o'clock, and a fine nicht," would start them up to hurry homewards. Some of the older lads warning their younger companions— "You'll catch't the nicht for bein' oot sae late."

Passing through Hanover Street into Miller Street, which then consisted chiefly of first class self-contained houses, but having no garden ground connected with them. On the west side behind Miller Street were here and there workshops, and tenements of respectable dwelling houses. Entering into a "through-gaun" close on one of these, leading into Queen Street, on the east side of which stood the coach building works and timber yard belonging to Mr. M'Lellan. A little below the sugar house already mentioned, on the west side of the street, nearly opposite, were the iron stores of Messrs. Kidston, while on the east side, next to the coach builders' yard, was a row of self-contained houses, having at one time had small garden plots in front, but now neglected, some of the houses now being occupied as offices, etc. Next to these were the workshops of Mr. William Scott, jappaner of tea trays, dial plates, and other fancy articles. At the upper end of his premises stood a very large tree, the branches of which overshadowed the street, beyond the pavement, and was often a very cool retreat for workmen at their meals on a hot summer day.

Next to Mr. Scott's was the coppersmith and brass foundry works of the Messrs. Wardrop, having a large yard and workshops, and employing a number of men in the manufacture of copper boilers, large and small, brass and copper articles of all kinds. Passing through a "pen" court a little further down was the entrance to an extensive cooperage, the windows of the workshop fronting the street, the lower part was closed in with a shutter to prevent passers by looking in on the men at their work. Through the same "pen" court was an entrance to the stores of Mr. James Lumsden, wholesale stationer, whose large front premises were immediately below this cooperage.

Passing along to the west, on the north side of Argyle Street, to the foot of Buchanan Street, on the west side stood the residence of Thomas Lightbody, surgeon, on the second floor, which was reached by an outside stone stair, projecting on the pavement. There were not many passengers, and it was not felt to be an inconvenience. The surgery was in an apartment fronting Argyle Street, in the window of which were a number of glass jars and bottles of all sizes, containing reptiles of various kinds, from a worm to a spiral serpent crushed into the largest bottle. In the centre was a large glass globe, filled with a liquid of a light green colour, behind which a lamp was kept burning, indicating the doctor's residence and casting a brilliant light across the street. It was often a guide to passengers, as the streets and lanes were then very dimly lighted with oil lamps, which during stormy winter evenings were often blown out, leaving the streets gloomy and dark, so that people going and returning in visiting friends, or other social gatherings, used to have a servant going before them, carrying a lantern to guide their steps in the sometimes not overly-clean portions of the streets.

STREETS FIRST LIGHTED WITH GAS.

Within about a year from this time, a very great change for the better was made on the streets, by the introduction of gas-light, and many a queer inquiry and remark was made about it on the first few nights after the Trongate was lighted up, when numerous groups came to see the new light, by many of whom the process was not very well understood—such as, " Whaur dis the lowe come frae ? " or " I' thae nae wick intilt ? " Others, thinking the flame came up through the metal pillar, would cautiously apply their hand to feel if it was hot ! while others kept to the " crown of the causeway," at a safe distance, as if fearing an explosion.

Next to the tenement in which Dr. Lightbody resided was the " Auld Kil," a large farm steading. Whether it derived the name from having at one time been used as a malt kiln, or from some other cause, is not known. The farm house stood about twelve feet back from the line of Argyle Street, one storey high, having high pitched roof covered with thatch, a small door and two windows in front; inside, a large " but and ben " below, and sleeping places above; behind were barn, stables, and byre. Some of these close on the side of St. Enoch's Burn, which ran open through the steading, under a small bridge across the street, and into the Burn Close.

What is now Mitchell Street was an irregular country lane, leading from the farm steading into open fields and on to the

village of Cowcaddens. Long before the adjoining streets were
opened up it was a busy thoroughfare. On the west side
from the corner of Argyle Street were a number of old tenements of various heights, with a small shop here and there.
Some of these buildings were three storeys in height, having an
entrance from the street by inside wooden stairs to the flats
above. These houses were chiefly occupied by the tradesmen
in the various works in the vicinity. Above these was an iron
foundry, for many years occupied by Blairs & Robinson, iron
founders, whose trade was chiefly in casting iron pillars, railings,
etc. Above the foundry was a very old thorn hedge, and an
open burn behind, extending to the end of the lane. On the
east of the lane or street were a variety of old stores, large and
small, in which all sorts of merchandise were stored—tradesmen's
yards, blacksmith shop, ashpits, etc., down to the side of St.
Enoch's Burn.

Passing along to Union Street, on the line of Argyle Street,
stood a range of old thatch houses, one storey in height, consisting of two or three dwelling houses, two small shops for the
sale of confections, vegetables, and "fruits in their seasons," etc.,
and a mechanic's workshop. Turning up into Union Street, on
the east side, and extending along more than the half of the
street, stood the extensive timber yard and workshops of Mr.
John Bennie. Next to these, separated by a narrow lane, was
the mahogany yard, cabinet workshop, and residence of Mr.
M'Ruer; then there was the Unitarian Chapel, a great resort
on winter Sabbath evenings for young lads and their sweet-
hearts, who went to hear the organ played.

There was no instrumental music used in any of the
churches or chapels throughout the city. The preachers of
the gospel of that day did not "need the foreign aid of orna-
ment" or instrument to attract the people to their churches,

the plain, earnest, affectionate preaching of the gospel filled, and often crowded the various churches in city and suburbs. There may have been instances, where some miserable, pitiful squabble among heritors, kirk session, and ministers, kept the church nearly empty, leaving the latter preaching to half filled and empty pews. This was rare. The churches were all well attended, and a pleasant, cheerful sight it was, on a quiet Sabbath day, to see the multitudes going along the streets to their various places of worship, without the slightest fear of being run over by cabs or tramcars. There were few cabs or noddys on the street, yet here and there might be seen sometimes a sedan chair, conveying an invalid, or a delicate mother with a child for baptism, or whatever they might believe to be a work of mercy.

HOW THE FIRST SUNDAY 'BUS WAS STARTED.

Previous to the year 1853 there were no omnibuses running on the streets on Sabbath. About that time a number of merchants and business men had taken up their residence in Partick, then a very pleasant village. These found it a hardship to travel in to their "ain kirk" in the city on Sabbath, and established an omnibus, only for taking people to and from church. It came in no further than York Street, and landed the passengers about a quarter of an hour before the time of service, giving the driver time to stable the horses and attend church. It was all very quiet, decent, and orderly, yet from this quiet but subtle beginning gradually arose a stream of Sabbath profanation, ever increasing, ever extending, on to the present day.

On the west side of Union Street, at the corner of Argyle Street, stood the milestone-like pillar, marking the then extended boundary of the city. Up from this, and about fifty feet back from the line of the street, were the backs of the houses in Grahamston, leaving a piece of neutral ground over which the police had no control. One or two tenements of first class houses had been erected at the upper end, still leaving a large space for housewives in Alston Street, whose houses were on that side, to take the advantage of this for bleaching clothes, coming out and in by their windows, which were about two feet from the ground, there being no opening or entrance from this side.

This was also a place where the schoolboys came to settle their quarrels, by fighting, as has often been done by mighty potentates and nations as well as by schoolboys. These quarrels arose out of such matters as to whose lead "pitcher was nearest the mug," while playing at the game of "muggie," or whose "bool" or "button" was nearest the mark, while playing at "ringie" or "pitch and toss;" or it might be a case of cheating. When a boy had picked up more "bools" or "buttons" than he was entitled to, arbiters were chosen, and if these did not agree, the disputants getting angry, a suggestion was made by an outsider that they should "fecht for't." "Yes, I'll fecht him, I've beat him at 'muggie' an' I'll beat him at fechtin' tae." "An' I'll haud the bonnet," shouted several voices. The boys always fought across a bonnet, held by two, one at each side, this prevented them getting into grips and hurting each other, and allowed either party to run away if his courage failed. Often a peaceable boy was brought into trouble in these cases through fear of being thought a coward.

On one of these occasions one of the combatants, when arrived on the ground, and who resided in Alston Street, had quite forgotten for the time that one of the windows of his mother's dwelling looked out on the battlefield; they had just begun to fight when she, hearing the noise, looked out, saw her son engaged in fighting, ran to the window, jumped out, rushed in amongst them, and, catching her son by the collar, dragged him in through the open window, "cuffing his chafts" as they went. The others scampered off to the school play-ground along with the other combatant, who was glad to get off so easily, saving his honour, without getting a thrashing from either the son or his mother.

Above and adjoining the tenements already referred to, stood the stores of the "Hurlet and Campsie Alum Company." It was a large brick building, extending from the line of Union Street nearly back to the houses in Grahamston, having the store-keeper's dwelling and offices on the front of the street. A branch of the Forth and Clyde Canal had now been opened up near to the village of Campsie, and the produce and manu-factures of that part of the country were now brought into Port-Dundas. This was then a very suitable position for the erection of the store ; the goods were sent from this by carriers to the various towns and villages where they were required.

CARRIERS AND CARRIERS' QUARTERS.

All the inland traffic throughout the whole country was then done by "carriers." At the corner of Ingram Street, on the east side of Brunswick Street, was the extensive establishment, or "Carriers Quarters," of Messrs. Hargreaves. This firm had a large number of waggons and carts constantly on the road, going to and from all parts of the coast and country, and it was a very lively scene as these carts and waggons arrived now and again, covering more than the half of Brunswick Street, opposite the "Quarters," unloading and loading the vehicles, and getting fresh horses and conductors started again on their journey.

Besides this, there were local carriers going daily, weekly, and twice a week, to Paisley, Greenock, Dumbarton, Hamilton, Lanark, and other towns and villages throughout the country. These all had their quarters in various parts of the city, suitable for the trade and the roads they were on; these carriers had a great traffic as letter-carriers. The postage of letters was then very high; to places at distances of such towns as already mentioned, the charge for a letter would be one shilling, more or less according to distance. People were not able to correspond with their friends at this rate, and a small parcel of coarse paper, folded into the size of a letter, and tied together, was given into the hands of the carrier, who took it, as a parcel, for a trifling sum of one or two pence.

The price of newspapers, as well as the rates of postage, were also very dear, 7d. to 8d. each (including government stamp), being the price for a newspaper of four pages, so that workmen and mechanics were not able to afford one for their own use. The wages of the working-classes, with few exceptions, being from thirteen to sixteen shillings per week of sixty hours; there was no uniform rate of wages, every man being paid according to his ability.

READING THE NEWSPAPERS—A PENNY AN HOUR.

In order to get a reading of the papers, some of which were published twice a week, economic plans had to be adopted. A news agent of those days would purchase, say a dozen or fifteen papers; these were lent out to clubs among shopkeepers and working men, the time arranged to suit the leisure or convenience of the respective parties, at the rate of a penny for two hours up till six o'clock in the evening, when the charge was one penny per hour from that up to ten o'clock. In many cases a few friendly neighbours in a tenement would arrange to have their papers in succession, and, meeting in each others houses, or, as often as could be got, in the house where there were no babies or young children to disturb the meeting, and getting a smart boy who could read well and distinctly, and who had patience to go straight through the matter, which, in general, was not very interesting to him till he came to a skirmish with the radicals, or a report that they were gathering in great numbers and marching into the city. By this means they each got three hours reading or hearing of the papers for their penny. The boy, whose services were well paid by a contribution of two or three "big pennies" now and again from his audience, would be sent to the shop of the preceding reader about a quarter before the hour, and would find him poring over the paper till the hour struck, then handed it to the boy, who hurried home to where the group were patiently, or often impatienty, waiting to hear of some startling event, which had been expected to take place for some time previous. These papers were collected by the newsagent on the following morning, and sold at half-price to small taverns and change-house keepers, for the use of their customers.

Next to the stores of the Hurlet and Campsie Alum Co. was a large extent of vacant ground, from the west of Grahamston, up to and beyond what was in later years Melville Street, on the north side of which a range of churches were erected—Burgher, Anti-Burgher, and Gaelic—extending from Renfield Street over to what is now Hope Street. Beyond this, to the north and west, as far as the village of Anderston, the various streets forming the new town were laid out at their proper height and declivity, leaving spaces between from six to twelve feet deep, according to the various heights of the original surface. In these large pools of water gathered during wet weather, and were much resorted to for sailing on rafts, when planks could be got for that purpose.

THE FIRST TELEPHONE.

The large plot of ground bordering on Grahamston was a playground and resort for all the apprentices and schoolboys residing there, and in Drury Lane and Mitchell Street there were often a number of large logs of timber laid down here from the yards on the opposite side, and among these were ample scope for all sorts of games—riding on planks, jumping over logs, etc.—and among these logs perhaps the germ of the future telephone may have been hid. There were, among the others, some very long logs of hardwood, and at either end of one of these some young girls had been quietly playing, and found that a very slight noise or scraping was heard distinctly at the other end. This led to further experiments, till it was found that the scratching of a pin could be heard distinctly. Some of the boys got notice of this, who, after trying it for themselves told it to others in this manner:—" I'll bet you a bool or a button that I'll let you hear a preen scratchin' at the en' o' that log," pointing to one of the longest. " Done!" He lost the bet, and gained it from the next who came upon the ground. This occupied the attention of the groups of players for a length of time, or till the long logs were removed, and matters of—to them—more importance took up their attention.

This plot of ground had always been disputed territory—those in Mitchell Street claimed an exclusive right to it ; while those in Grahamston held it to be theirs, as it was nearest to them. This—as among savage and civilised powers down from early ages on to the present time—led to continuous quarrels, which resulted in " stone battles," in which the lads in Grahamston had the advantage—they having a large territory behind the village to which they could retreat ; and so bitter was the feeling between the parties during these hostilities that a boy or lad from Grahamston having occasion to go into or pass through Mitchell Street, without a protector, was sure to be set upon and beaten. These localities were at and beyond the extreme boundaries of the city. A policeman was seldom seen, so that there was no public authority on the streets to interfere and prevent those boyish outrages.

GREAT EXCITEMENT—A BIG FIRE.

The only times when policemen were seen in this vicinity was during the progress of a fire—more than one of which took place in and around Mitchell Street. One of the most serious of these, at that time, occurred a few years after this, or about 1828, by which a very large range of stores at the corner of Mitchell Lane were quite destroyed. The fire began about half-past eight o'clock in the evening, and brought together a very large crowd of people, who were then thronging the streets at that hour. The superintendent of police was Captain Graham, who always did his duties on horseback whenever circumstances allowed him to do so. On this occasion he was present on horseback, with a number of police to keep order and prevent the people from pressing too close upon the men engaged in attempting to extinguish the fire. With the help of the horse and two or three of the police he was able to do this, and keep a clear space on the street in front of the burning building. There were, however, a great number of people—men and young lads—who had got possession of the roofs of stables, sheds, and the tops of walls, from the corner of Gordon Street down nearly to the building. These he tried to remove from their position, sometimes by threats and sometimes by coaxing, but could not. Not having a sufficient number of men to spare from their duties at the fire, in order to remove them by force, he was at a loss what to do. At length a bright •

idea came into his mind. He rode down, and, after a brief consultation with some of the bystanders connected with the stores, galloped over to the crowds seated on the walls, shouting, "Gentlemen, come down, for —— there is a large quantity of gunpowder in the stores. The moment the fire reaches it you will all be blown to destruction." The *gentlemen* did not move, but sat quietly watching the progress of the fire, ready to come down whenever they saw the least indication of alarm on the part of the Captain and his men.

The mode of giving notice when a fire took place at this time was with the watchman's "clappers" and the "fire drum." These instruments were alarming enough without a fire, especially if they required to be played upon throughout the course of a winter night. When a fire took place in any part of the city, it was the duty of the watchman on that beat to take the name of the street and the number of the premises, then to hurry on towards the beat of the next watchman, "rattlin' his clappers" and shouting as he went, "Fire! fire! in No. ——, —— Street." The cry was taken up by his next neighbour, and so on, until the tidings reached the police station in Bell Street. The fire drum and drummer was at once sent out, hurrying through the principal streets drumming, and shouting as he went, "Fire in No. ——, —— Street!" The watchmen on the various beats took up the cry; and, in a very short space of time, the whole city was wakened up to know there was a fire at such a number, in such a street. This made those interested in the locality start up and hurry off to look after their property or premises. Besides the one or more fire-engines and water-butts that were always kept ready at the station—and which were sent off immediately—there were other engines kept in various parts of the city having premises located in the immediate vicinity or at a short distance. These, on hearing the cry, would start up and hurry off with their engine to the scene of the fire ; when, if the fire happened to be of a trifling nature and their services not required, they would at once return to their stations. The farthest out of these stations toward the west was on the south side of Argyle Street, opposite to the village of Grahamston.

PUBLIC WHIPPINGS.

Other calm, but more exciting, scenes had often taken place on the streets of old Glasgow, when, in former years, punishment of criminals by public whipping through the streets was not a rare occurrence ; when, amidst the breathless silence of the crowd, not a sound was heard for a brief space of time save only the sound of the lash on the back of the criminal. It was a brutal-looking, but perhaps a wholesome, punishment in many cases. The last of these public whippings took place somewhere about the year 1819. It was for a gross case of assault and rape on a young woman—then a capital crime. The culprit was stripped naked down to below the waist, and firmly tied to the hind bar of a common cart, and walking along with it to the various places where a portion of the number of stripes for which sentence had been given were to be laid on. On arriving at the head of Stockwell Street, which was one of these places, on the way to the Cross, where the last portion of the punishment was to be inflicted, the culprit's back was in a sorely lacerated condition, and painful to look upon. It might be difficult to say what would be the varied feelings of the spectators of the scene. Perhaps the remark of an old woman, who was standing with some neighbours at a "close mouth" on the south side of Trongate, would indicate the feelings of the majority. She had been looking on with quiet satisfaction while the lash was being laid on ; and, as the procession moved away, turned to a neighbour at her side, remarking to this effect :—"Eh, Mrs. T., A was sair, sair vext for the last puir chiel that A saw whuppit through the streets o' Glesca ; A canna say what it was for—something aboot pollytiks or treesun, or something or ither o' that kind o' thing ; A was wae, wae for him, and cou'd hae grutten richt oot ; but this yin, I'm no yae hair vext for him. To gae wa' an' mis-use an' abuse the inecent lassie, the blagyert that he wus ; it's a gude thing they didna hang him. Hanging wud been owre gude for him, the scoon-er-all that he is."

THE KING'S BIRTHDAY.

But, of all the exciting scenes that took place in the city for many years, none were more so than the annual celebration of the King's Birthday. There were very seldom any very riotous demonstrations, but a calm, cool determination on the part of about a third of the population to show their loyalty by burning tar-barrels and making bonfires, the materials for which were generally got from public property, while the whole population took part, more or less, in the general display, and the more unworthy the reigning monarch might be, the more mischief was done to honour him.

The juvenile part of the population took a deep interest in these celebrations, it being a sort of holiday in most of the schools, and a day in which they had a little license to use gun-powder, more or less, according to the feelings and circum-stances of parents and guardians. This license was often carried to excess. From early morning small metal cannons, mounted on carriages, were brought out ; while by those who were not so fortunate as to have any of these, every article of metal that could be formed into anything that would make a noise or report was brought into play. Some of these had a tendency to discharge at the wrong end, to the sometimes

danger of the hand that held it, while scorched eyebrows and
singed hair, got by blowing the spark in a piece of cotton, to
explode a quantity of powder, were often to be seen. There
were, however, some serious accidents occurred through careless-
ness. One of these took place in Drury Lane to a young
black boy, who had come from one of the West Indian Islands
with his father, a coloured man, a servant in attendance upon a
merchant from that island. Being in lodgings, he was left very
much to himself, and having some coppers allowed him for other
purposes, spent them on gunpowder (being quite a new thing to
him), which, for convenience in amusing himself with, he emptied
into the outside pocket of his jacket, putting a piece of cotton
in beside it. There had been a spark in the cotton, which in a
short time ignited the powder, and the whole blew up, injuring
the arm and shoulder very severely. The father had been out
of town, in attendance on his master, and was not aware of the
acciden to his boy till the returned two days after. He at once
rushed to see his boy, and it was a sight to see the father and
son meeting, and the fond embraces and joy of the parent to
find that, serious as the accident had been, it was not so very
bad as he had been led to believe.

During the day, here and there throughout the city, the
reports of the juvenile firearms were heard, on till evening, when
the crowds began to gather in the Trongate and Argyle Street,
parties of whom began to make preparations for bonfires at the
Cross and at the head of Stockwell Street. It would be difficult
to say where the materials forming these came from. Private
property, not properly protected, suffered to a certain extent.
The chief supply came from the enclosures round about the
Green, which were then almost wholly composed of rough
timber fences. While the fires were being kindled, processions
were formed, tar barrels procured — honestly, or otherwise ;

these, carried shoulder-high on long wooden rafters, were set on fire and carried through the streets, and then thrown on the fires, the heat from which was on some occasions so intense as to blister the paint of the woodwork of the shops at the Cross. While these proceedings were going on in the street, there was a continuous discharge of fireworks of all descriptions from the windows of the houses above. Altogether it was a very lively scene for a few hours, extending from Anderston Walk on to the Cross.

These annual celebrations generally passed off peaceably, and if at any time there were indications of rioting, a band of special constables, armed with batons, who had been previously sworn in for the occasion, were called out to preserve order, and a few of the regular police, mixing among the crowds, carried boards, on which were inscribed, " The Riot Act has been read." These precautions kept the crowd in check, and by about eleven o'clock the respectable portion had returned home, and between twelve and one the streets were perfectly quiet, with the exception of a few stragglers.

Returning again to Grahamston and the disputed playground, on the west side of which, and fronting to Alston Street, were two large old granaries, or stores for grain. These were the first granaries erected in or around the city. The reason for these being placed in this then out-of-the-way village was the forma-tion and opening up of the Forth and Clyde Canal and its branches. This canal was commenced in July, 1768; but, owing to much opposition, want of funds, and other causes, was not finished till 1790, when it was opened with much ceremony, a hogshead of water from the River Forth having been brought and emptied into the River Clyde, at Bowling, with many cere-monials and amidst great rejoicing. A branch of the canal had been carried on to what is now Port-Dundas, where stores and

warehouses were erected, and merchandise brought into the city
by Port-Dundas Road.   These two granaries were erected here,
as being the nearest point to this road, and immediately beyond
the boundary of the city.

On the west side of Alston Street, and nearly opposite to
these granaries, stood the sugar-house, or sugar refinery, and a
little west from this, where the Corn Exchange now stands, was
a small piece of marshy ground, or ditch.   On the edge of this
willow bushes had been planted, and yielded a continual supply
of "willow whauns" for making creels and baskets used by the
market gardeners.   Beyond this to the west, and up toward
the north, was a large space of garden ground, which had, a few
years previous, been enclosed and divided by low stone walls,
but was now in a ruinous and neglected state, owing to the
great mass of earth laid down on the grounds while forming the
streets of the New Town.   These grounds were much frequented
in summer and winter evenings by young men and boys from
the villages of Brownfield and Grahamston, and from Drury
Lane.

FIRE-BALOONING.

In the winter it was a favourite amusement preparing and
setting off fiery balloons, some of them very large.   They were
made of fine silk paper, tapering towards the bottom, round
which was a light wire hoop, having a hook in the middle, on
which a sponge dipped in turpentine was hung and set fire to
after the balloon had been inflated over the smoke of a fire.
Some of these balloons often went up a great height and distance,
and the greatest excitement among the crowd of youths who
had been watching the proceedings was the running off in all
directions, calculating where it might fall, and be the first to
catch it.

This practice of balloon-flying prevailed over the country for a length of time, until it was discovered that several fires of haystacks, thatch houses, etc., had been caused by their descent upon them while the flame in the sponge was still burning. This led to a strict Government inquiry being made, and the result was the passing of a law which made it a serious crime, and put an end to balloon-flying in Grahamston, and over the whole country.

In the summer seasons these grounds were much frequented, for the purpose of flying kites, on the raised ground forming the proposed streets, and in the hollows between, playing the game of rounders, putting stones, playing quoits, etc. The kites were of all shapes and sizes, from the halfpenny one bought in the shops, up to the large kite ten feet high, strongly put together, and requiring two young men to hold it in when it reached the great height to which it attained, notwithstanding the great weight of strong cord attached to it.

PLAYING AT SAVAGES.

Another recreation was the erecting, or, rather, the digging out of what was called "Fair o' Glesca houses," to be used at the Fair Holiday. Eight or ten young lads would unite together, to form one of these, which was considered to be their own property. They were about nine feet diameter at the top, tapering down to about seven or eight feet at bottom, and about five feet deep, raised to about six feet by a wall of earth to throw off the water, and roofed over with old planks, paling-stobs, or whatever could be got. These, covered with straw or turf, over which a thick coat of earth was laid, made quite a water-tight house. They laboured very earnestly at them for two or three weeks before the Fair days, and then, and for many days after, were used as a sort of club-room, to which they could retreat

4

and enjoy themselves during wet weather.   These houses were
sometimes destroyed during the summer by parties in search of
planks which had been *borrowed* for the purpose of joining the
roofs, but were again fitted-up on the approach of New-Year's
Day, having a snug and cosy little fireplace on one side ; and
here, during the long winter evenings, the groups often assembled to tell stories, club together their pence, cook and feast on
potatoes and herrings, etc., and thoroughly enjoy themselves
without any stimulant, only a bottle of small beer now and
again, at a halfpenny a bottle, purchased from some of the lads'
mothers, who generally kept a stock on hand for porridge at
breakfast.   If at any time, while forming underground railways,
etc., the workmen, at a depth of about twenty-five feet, should
come upon a heap of ashes mixed with burned bones, an iron
grating, a black bottle, a brown jug, a gully knife, a two-pronged
fork, and perhaps a copper coin or two, antiquarians need not
puzzle about them—they are only the remains of what were, at
one time, Fair o' Glesca houses.

TAXING THE DAYLIGHT.

These recreation grounds were gradually done away with as
building operations progressed in the vicinity, about 1821. The
first of these, on this plot of ground, was a building immediately
opposite to Drury Lane, on the west side of what is now
Renfield Street.   It was the City Cess Office, two storeys in
height, having the collector's house in front and entrance to
the offices by the south side.   This was where all government
taxes were paid for some years.   Taxation at this time was
very heavy on the people, and some of these very grievous; and
none more so than the tax on windows—or " window lichts," as
it was called—a tax on all windows in every dwelling, even one-
room houses, of which there were very few at that time.   It was

felt to be very grievous among the working classes, with their then very low wages, and gave rise to many a bitter outcry, and even sympathy with the foolish Radical attempt to overthrow the government by force.   This tax was often spoken of in substance such as this : that while all the gifts of God to sinful fallen man were free—without money or without price—our presumptuous, tyrannical government would not allow His sun to shine, nor air to enter, even into the dwellings of the poor, without its being paid for.

COCK-FIGHTING.

Two or three years after this, another encroachment was made on the play-ground farther west, by the opening up of Hope Street into Argyle Street.   The buildings on the west side of this street were on, and formed the boundary of, Grahamston.   For a few years after the opening of this street, the ground on either side at the lower end, on to about 1830, was entirely covered with workshops of various trades—large and small; although doubts were sometimes expressed that they were going too far west from the city.   Among those on the west side was a large horse-shoeing and veterinary establishment.   There were often to be seen going out and in about these premises numbers of well-dressed people, and others of less reputable appearance, apparently engaged in looking after the horses; but it was not known to the public—only to those who were directly or indirectly engaged in the business— that a cock-pit had been formed in the back premises, and that here parties met from time to time to engage in the brutal practice of cock-fighting.

When this cock-pit was about to be fitted up, three or four years after the erection of the premises, by a wright and builder occupying large premises a little farther west, he came to one of his workmen and was proceeding to describe the work, giving him instructions to proceed with it ; the man very respectfully, but firmly, declined to do the work. The employer was astonished, and said rather angrily, " There's nobody wantin' you to fecht the cocks ! " The other said it would be doing all in his power to assist others to " fecht them." After a few remarks, the employer left him, to give the job to others less scrupulous, seeming pleased he had a workman who had refused to fit up a cock-pit.

A FAMOUS D.D. IN THOSE DAYS.

It was about the same time that Hope Street was opened up that the three churches already referred to began to be built; and granaries on the south side, forming a street on the line of Gordon Street, on to Hope Street, which was then named Melville Street. The church in the centre, directly opposite Alston Street, was that of Dr. Beattie, then one of the United Secession Churches, now the United Presbyterian. Dr. Beattie was an earnest, powerful preacher ; the church was always well filled by members and adherents, many of whom belonged to or were residenters in Grahamston. He was, in general, very faithful in his discourses ; but on one or two occasions rather failed in this. Once, in particular, while preaching on the " Sanctity of the Sabbath," and describing very minutely the various ways in which the Sabbath was being profaned, he took no notice of parties who used their own or hired carriages for conveyance on Sabbath—which was then considered a very serious violation of the command, and gave great offence to his people—as it was considered to be through fear of, or in deference to, one of his members (Mr. Smith) moving in rather higher social circles than the others, who, on the occasion of the baptism of his children, and in stormy weather and other circumstances, drove to the church in a cab or carriage of his own. One of his daughters was Madeline Smith, who in after years was tried before the Court in Edinburgh on a charge of having caused the death of her sweetheart, a young Frenchman, by poisoning. This trial—although the charge was not proved against her—caused a very great excitement throughout the whole country, and especially in Edinburgh and Glasgow, where her grandfather and father were well known and moving in a respectable position in society, for whom, for her, and the whole family much sympathy was felt.

On another occasion the Doctor gave rather serious offence to a number of his members, or, rather, confirmed them in what he considered a great evil they were about to commit, in. the formation of a Christian Instruction Society in the church. This was about five or six years after the Glasgow City Mission was established, and was intended to work in the same manner as they were doing, visiting from house to house and preaching the Gospel, and helping the poor in the neglected districts in the locality around the church and elsewhere. This rather offended the Doctor, as if it had indicated a want on his part, although there was no such feeling, and led him to preach a sermon on the subject, taking for his text, "I magnify mine office," in which he brought out the dignity and importance of the ministerial office, and the evils that would arise from the doctrines of the Gospel being taught by men who had not the necessary learning, etc., and so on. It had no effect. The society was formed and flourished, and there was no more said about the dignity of the ministerial office. Notwithstanding matters such as these, Dr. Beattie was much esteemed by his people, and many were much benefited during the course of his ministrations among them.

THE SUGAR-HOUSE IN GRAHAMSTON.

The sugar-house already referred to was the farthest-up building on the west side of Alston Street, and beyond it was a space of ground, partly enclosed, on which all the rubbish, ashes, broken sugar-moulds, etc., were deposited. This depository was a great resort for boys and girls and young lads, to gather out the broken sugar-moulds from among the rubbish ; these, being thoroughly saturated with sugar, were a sort of sweetmeat that was highly relished. Some of these youngsters made a trade out of this, and hawked it all round the various localities as "sugar mug," selling it for preens, bools, and buttons, these articles being traded with again—preens and buttons to thrifty housewives, and bools to schoolboys. If at any time the supply from the sugar-house failed, these enterprising young scoundrels would collect broken flower-pots and roofing tiles, selling these as genuine "sugar mug," and leaving the victims to suck at these till the tongue was sore, in the vain attempt to extract saccharine matter out of them.

This sugar-house would be erected about the year 1808 ; it was a building of six storeys in height, but very narrow in proportion to the great height. At the south end was the engine-house and stalk from the flues of the boiler, rising eight or ten feet above the gable.

THE TERRIBLE FALL OF THE SUGAR-HOUSE.

This building was the scene of a terrible calamity when, on the morning of 2nd November, 1848, it fell, or rather crumbled down into a ruinous heap, without giving any warning, causing the death of twelve out of the eighteen men employed at the works, leaving only the south gable standing, which, being supported by the engine-house, stood erect. The fall of the building caused a great consternation and excitement in the neighbourhood, and numbers of workmen from the timber-yards and workshops, which had now for some years been erected on Blythswood grounds, at once hurried to the scene of disaster to render assistance, but little could be done. The side walls and north gable had mostly all fallen inwardly, leaving a mass of closely-packed building materials, which took some days to remove, although by the 6th, or four days after the building fell, all the bodies had been got out except one. Much sympathy was felt throughout the city for the families of the sufferers, and by the 10th a sum of £400 had been subscribed for their benefit.

It was believed that the sugar-house had been in a very insecure state for some years, owing to the quantity of steam arising during the process of sugar refining, and the constant vibration of the machinery used for various purposes throughout the building had affected the walls, rendering them liable to fall in the manner they did, though still outwardly having every appearance of stability.

The sugar-house was not again built in this locality, there being a great demand for ground for the erection of granaries. From near the corner of Union Street, down both sides of Alston Street, along Melville Street, and down the east side of Hope Street, had now been built upon with these, besides others in the near locality, and as there were great quantities of grain from all quarters now coming in at the Broomielaw, granaries and stores had been and were still being built, to meet the demand for storage. Washington Street had, some years before this, been opened up, and flour mills established there; large stores had been erected on the west side of York Street, and at the corners of Argyle and James Watt Streets.

IN MEMORY OF JAMES WATT.

The ground on which this street was formed had been acquired by a nephew of the celebrated James Watt—the discoverer of the power of steam, and the practicability of its being applied to the working of machinery, and was named so by him in honour of his uncle. In all the changes taking place in the locality around, the village of Grahamston still retained much of its primitive character; all the market gardeners had left, their occupation in this part of the city was gone, and the neat, well-kept kitchen gardens were now no longer to be seen, their places in the village being filled up with store-keepers and granary-men. These being, generally, quiet, sober men, there was never any brawling or noisy behaviour on the street, with the exception of one court at the lower end, where a large public-house had been for some time established, having back entrances from the court. The street of the village never became a great thoroughfare, and the inhabitants of the upper part still enjoyed their quiet summer evenings out of doors, as formerly. It was, however, made a very quiet thoroughfare on Sabbath at the hours of worship, for people going to and returning from the churches in the immediate vicinity—the Gaelic church, Dr. Beattie's, Dr. Willis', and the Independent Tabernacle in Drury Lane. The latter of these was removed many years since, to make way for business premises, Dr. Beattie's being the first to remove to an elevated position towards the north-west. Dr. Willis' was the next to remove, and gradually what was, not many years ago, the playground and the battlefield of groups of young children and lads, full of merriment and mischief, was now covered with business premises, offices, etc., until all that was once connected with Grahamston was swept away, and the once pleasant, quiet, rural village also blotted out, and buried under the Central Railway and station.

What a sad and lamentable change has now taken place over the whole locality! Where once the multitudes were gathering together from every direction on the morning of the Sabbath, to worship God in His sanctuary, now, on the same holy Sabbath, may be seen crowds hurrying from every direction to catch the train, that carries them swiftly away from the worship of God. Where once the father and mother were seen, gently and tenderly leading their children up to the house of God, may now, sometimes, be seen among the crowds, the impatient father hurrying his children along, lest they should be too late to catch the train.

AND NOW "LET GLASGOW FLOURISH."

It has already been said that during the last seventy years Glasgow has flourished and extended more than in all its previous history. May our flourishing second city still continue to flourish, not by the running of Sabbath trains, not by the unhallowed sapping of the foundations of the city, and forming subterranean vaults to extend that traffic; but, " Let Glasgow Flourish by the Preaching of the Word."

THE END.

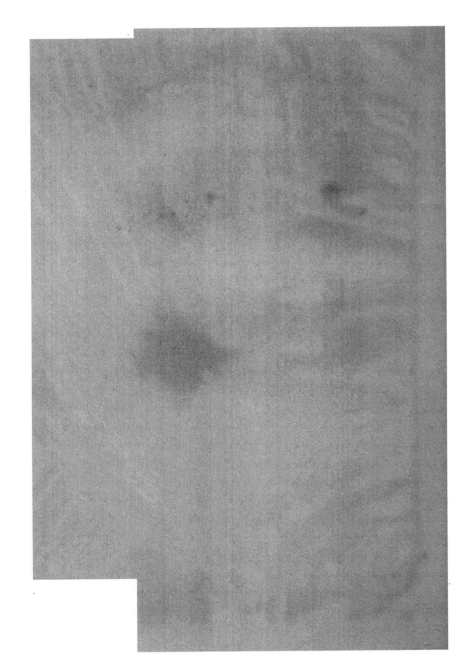